T0195811

CHRIST BEFORE BETHLEHEM

*Old Testament Appearances of the
Preincarnate Jesus Christ*

RAYMOND HORNE

WESTBOW
PRESS®
A DIVISION OF THOMAS NELSON
& ZONDERVAN

WestBow Press books may be ordered through booksellers or by contacting:

WestBow Press
A Division of Thomas Nelson & Zondervan
1663 Liberty Drive
Bloomington, IN 47403
www.westbowpress.com
1 (866) 928-1240

ISBN: 978-1-9736-7307-1 (sc)
ISBN: 978-1-9736-7308-8 (e)

Library of Congress Control Number: 2019913753

Print information available on the last page.

WestBow Press rev. date: 10/10/2019

Who can find an excellent wife?
She is far more precious than jewels.
—Proverbs 31:10 (HCSB)

To my darling wife, Janice. She was and is a beautiful blessing from God. She is a rare and precious jewel that my heart was blessed to find. I praise God for the fifty years we have shared as husband and wife. This book would have been impossible without her encouragement and support.

CONTENTS

INTRODUCTION

My favorite time of the year is the Christmas season. I love the focus Christmas gives to the birth of Jesus Christ. One of my favorite Christmas carols is a beautiful Appalachian ballad written by William Howard Doane (1832–1915), titled "Christ Was Born in Bethlehem."[1] The first verse says:

> Christ was born in Bethlehem, Christ was born in Bethlehem.
> Christ was born in Bethlehem and in a manger lay.
> And in a manger lay, and in a manger lay,
> Christ was born in Bethlehem and in a manger lay.

Yes, Christ was born in Bethlehem and in a manger lay, but Christ's existence didn't begin with His coming to this earth as a baby in Bethlehem. Christ existed before Bethlehem. The apostle John emphasized this in the beginning of his Gospel: "In the beginning was the Word (Jesus), and the Word was with God, and the Word was God. He was in the beginning with God. All things were made through Him, and without Him nothing was made that was made" (John 1:1-3, ESV).

The apostle Paul also affirms this truth in the book of Colossians: "The Son is the image of the invisible God, the firstborn over all creation. For in him all things were created: things in heaven and on earth, visible and invisible, whether thrones or powers or rulers or authorities; all things have been created through him and for him. He is before all things, and in him all things hold together" (Colossians 1:15–17).

Jesus was present at the beginning of creation. He was and is our creator. His preexistence is further affirmed by His many appearances documented throughout the Old Testament. Theophany is a theological word that refers to an encounter with God prior to Christ's incarnation.

The *Holman Bible Dictionary* tells us that "The phenomena of theophanies were temporary, for the occasion that required them, and then disappeared. On the other hand, in the incarnate Christ His deity and humanity were joined, not for time alone, but for eternity."[2]

However, in the early days of humanity, before men had the written Word, before the incarnation, and before the Holy Spirit had come to make His abode in human hearts, God sometimes appeared and talked with men. Before man sinned, he walked and talked with God, but after sin entered, Adam and his wife hid when they heard the voice of God (Genesis 3:8). God spoke to Cain (Genesis 4) and Enoch (Genesis 5:24), and Noah "walked with God" (Genesis 6:9). There is good reason to think that theophanies before the incarnation of Christ were in fact visible manifestations of the preincarnate Son of God. It is to be noticed that theophanies ceased with the incarnation of our Lord.[3]

So, only in the Old Testament economy did God's people need a theophany; since the incarnation, there is no such necessity. The New Testament doctrine of God is final and complete. God is always present in the risen Christ and the Holy Spirit. Still, at times, God's people are more aware of that presence than at others.[4]

The word theophany is a combination of two Greek words, *theos*, which means "God," and *epiphaneia*, which means "a shining forth" or "appearance."[5]

A Christophany is specifically an Old Testament appearance of Christ, the second person of the Trinity. Since no one has seen or can see God the Father (Exodus 33:20; John 1:18, 5:37, 6:46; 1 Timothy 6:15–16), most theologians believe the times in the Old Testament where God is "seen" refer to Jesus.[6]

Dr. John Walvoord, in his great book *Jesus Christ Our Lord,* makes the following statement about these Old Testament appearances: "It is safe to assume that every visible manifestation of God in bodily form in the Old Testament is to be identified with the Lord Jesus Christ."[7]

Some of the theophanies are found in these passages:

1. **Genesis 12:7–9**. The Lord appeared to Abraham on his arrival in the land God had promised to him and his descendants.
2. **Genesis 18:1–33**. One day, Abraham had some visitors: two angels and God Himself. He invited them to come to his home, and he and Sarah entertained them. Many commentators believe this could also be a Christophany, a preincarnate appearance of Christ.
3. **Genesis 32:22–30**. Jacob wrestled with what appeared to be a man but was actually God (vv. 28–30). This may also have been a Christophany.
4. **Exodus 3:2–4:17**. God appeared to Moses in the form of a burning bush, telling him exactly what He wanted him to do.
5. **Exodus 24:9–11**. God appeared to Moses with Aaron and his sons and the seventy elders.
6. **Deuteronomy 31:14–15**. God appeared to Moses and Joshua in the transfer of leadership to Joshua.
7. **Job 38–42**. God answered Job out of the tempest and spoke at great length in answer to Job's questions.

Frequently, the term "glory of the Lord" reflects a theophany, as in Exodus 24:16–18; the "pillar of cloud" has a similar function in Exodus 33:9. A frequent introduction for theophanies may be seen in the words "the Lord came down," as in Genesis 11:5, Exodus 34:5, and Numbers 11:5 and 12:5.

Many Bible commentators believe that whenever someone received a visit from "the angel of the Lord," this was in fact the preincarnate Christ.

There has only ever been one incarnation of God, Jesus of Nazareth, and there is no other. Incarnation means truly the fruit of a woman's womb—that is, fully human yet truly God Almighty … for in him dwells all the fullness of the Godhead bodily (Colossians 2:9, ESV).

Yet the people who saw these appearances believed that they were seeing God and hearing His voice, not angels.

Example: Jacob said that he saw and wrestled with God, who came to him in the form of a man (Genesis 32:30).

Example: Abraham's experience with the three men described in Genesis 18. He clearly tells of the Lord speaking with him face-to-face as a man, and then as a man who sat with him and shared a meal with him. After talking, He walked off.

Example: Joshua fell down and worshipped an "angel," and the angel didn't forbid him from worshipping Him, which he should have done if He was only an angel (Joshua 5:14, 15).

Example: Gideon said that he spoke with the angel of the Lord (Judges 6:11–24), yet he refers to the words of the "angel" as being the Lord's voice. Angel means messenger, so, while the Son of God is not an angel, those who witnessed His appearances were not wrong in saying that He was a messenger/angel of God (while He's not an angel).

Example: Moses at the burning bush in Exodus 3. In chapters 23, 32, and 33, God tells Moses that He will send His angel before him and that He has put His name in Him.

Isaiah 63:9 tells us, "And the angel of His presence saved them (the Israelites); in His love and in His pity, He redeemed them; and He bare them, and carried them all the days of old" (ESV).

First Corinthians 10:3–4 reminds us as well, "They all ate the same spiritual food and drank the same spiritual drink; for they drank from the spiritual rock that accompanied them, and that rock was Christ."

Example: The mysterious Melchizedek.

> This Melchizedek was king of Salem and priest of God
> Most High. He met Abraham returning from the defeat of

the kings and blessed him, and Abraham gave him a tenth of everything. First, the name Melchizedek means "king of righteousness"; then also, "king of Salem" means "king of peace." Without father or mother, without genealogy, without beginning of days or end of life, resembling the Son of God, he remains a priest forever. (Hebrews 7:1–3)

Example: The fourth man of Daniel 3:25, "I see four men loose, walking in the midst of the fire, and they have no hurt; and the form of the fourth is like the Son of God." Who told Nebuchadnezzar that there was a Son of God?

If you go through the concordance listing of the "Angel of the Lord," in some cases, this angel speaks in the first person as God. Some cults say, "See! that proves that Jesus is only an angel." No, it doesn't. Because the word *angel* simply means messenger or representative, it can have several applications.

Now, here's the point. The actual angelic angels that we sometimes entertain unawares are not incarnating when they drop in on us for a cup of coffee or if we pick them up as hitchhikers. In such occurrences, they are not incarnating as flesh and blood and then switching back to a spiritual body afterward, when they—poof—disappear. By the power of God, they are manifesting/materializing, to all appearances, to be men while not being men. It's a non-incarnation. God can do it, no problem. In a similar way, the Son of God was manifest in the appearance of a man several times in the Old Testament while not being a man or an angel, and this happened before His incarnation. This explains the Christophanies that I listed above. Just as angels can change their glorious form and appearance to such an extent that we can't tell them from any other Joe on the street, so did the all-glorious Son of God change His appearance, and He appeared on the earth at times before the days of His flesh.

God has always been vitally interested in the affairs of people on earth. He is so interested, in fact, that He has appeared numerous times to help humankind in the fight against evil.

Again, most Bible scholars believe that the Lord Jesus Himself appeared on earth several times before He came as a baby in Bethlehem. The name for these preincarnate appearances of Jesus is Christophanies.

Following is list of twenty of the Christophanies of Jesus (appearances before He came as a baby in Bethlehem), as recorded in the Old Testament:

Bible reference: Genesis 12:1–9
Appeared to: Abraham
Action: Abraham's call

Bible reference: Genesis 16:1–16
Appeared to: Hagar
Action: Instructed Hagar to return to Sarah and told her she would have many descendants.

Bible reference: Genesis 18
Appeared to: Abraham
Action: Jesus tells Abraham that Sarah will have a son and that Sodom will be destroyed.

Bible reference: Genesis 22:11–13
Appeared to: Abraham
Action: Abraham is prevented from sacrificing his son, Isaac.

Bible reference: Genesis 32: 24–30
Appeared to: Jacob
Action: The messenger wrestled with Jacob through the night and blesses him at daybreak.

Bible reference: Exodus 3:1–4:17
Appeared to: Moses
Action: Jesus appears to Moses in the burning bush with the command to go to Egypt and deliver Israel.

Bible reference: Exodus 14:19–20
Appeared to: Israelites

Action: Jesus protected the children of Israel from the pursuing Egyptian army.

Bible reference: Exodus 20:20–23
Appeared to: Israelites
Action: Jesus prepares the children of Israel to enter the Promised Land.

Bible reference: Numbers 22:23–35
Appeared to: Balaam
Action: Jesus appeared to Balaam, a rebellious prophet.

Bible reference: Joshua 5:13–6:27
Appeared to: Joshua
Action: Jesus appeared to Joshua as he contemplated the attack on Jericho.

Bible reference: Judges 2:1–5
Appeared to: Israelites
Action: Jesus appeared with a message of the consequences of their disobedience.

Bible reference: Judges 6:11–24
Appeared to: Gideon
Action: Jesus appeared to cowardly Gideon, one of the fearful Jews who was harassed by the Midianites.

Bible reference: 1 Kings 19:4–8
Appeared to: Elijah
Action: Jesus provided food for Elijah in the wilderness.

Bible reference: Judges 13
Appeared to: Manoah's wife
Action: Jesus appears to Manoah's wife with the prophesy of the conception of a son though she was sterile.

Bible reference: 1 Chronicles 21:16–22
Appeared to: David

Action: Jesus appeared to David on the threshing floor of Ornan, where David built an altar.

Bible reference: Isaiah 37:36
Appeared to: residents of Jerusalem
Action: Jesus delivered the citizens of Jerusalem.

Bible reference: Daniel 3:25
Appeared to: Shadrach, Meshach, and Abednego
Action: Jesus was there in the fiery furnace.

Bible reference: Daniel 10
Appeared to: Daniel
Action: The glorified Christ appeared to Daniel with a detailed prophesy of the end-times.

Bible reference: Zechariah 12:10–14
Appeared to: Zachariah
Action: Jesus appeared to Zachariah to pronounce the return of the Jews from seventy years' captivity and the rebuilding of the temple.

Bible reference: Malachi 3:1
Appeared to: Malachi
Action: The "Messenger of the Covenant" comes in judgment.

Now, let's dig in a little deeper as we look at eight Christophanies, eight Old Testament appearances of Jesus Christ before Bethlehem. We will begin with Christ's appearance to Abraham.

CHAPTER 1

CHRIST APPEARS TO ABRAHAM

Genesis 12:1–9

Now the Lord said to Abram, "Go forth from your country,
And from your relatives
And from your father's house,
To the land which I will show you;
And I will make you a great nation,
And I will bless you,
And make your name great;
And so, you shall be a blessing;
And I will bless those who bless you,
And the one who curses you I will curse.
And in you all the families of the earth shall be
blessed" (NAS).
So, Abram went.
—Genesis 12:1–4

Abram, whose name was later changed to Abraham, was the son of Terah, a descendent of Shem, and a native of Ur. After receiving God's call, Abraham entered the Promised Land undergirded by his faith in this covenant promise of God. He is described as the friend of God (2 Chronicles 20:7), a man of faith and prayer (Genesis 15:6; 18:23–33), and a man determined to be obedient to the Lord, whatever the cost (Genesis 22:1–18; Hebrews 11:8–10).

When God made this promise, Abraham had no son. But from Abraham, the Jewish nation would be born. God's promise was to make Abraham's name great and to bless him. This promise was fulfilled in Abraham's temporal blessings (13:2; 24:35), in Abraham's spiritual blessings (21:22), and in Abraham's fame (23:6; Isaiah 41:8). Abraham's relationship to God was so close that to bless Abraham was to bless God, and to curse Abraham was to curse God. We see examples of this in Genesis 20:2–18; 21:22–34; and 23:1–20.

God's promise was fulfilled to Abraham imminently in the coming of his son, Isaac, and eternally through the coming of Jesus Christ from Abraham's seed (Galatians 3:8, 16). Jesus is the "seed" who provides salvation for all people.

Abraham departed as the Lord had directed him. Abraham was seventy-five years old when he left Haran in obedience to God's call. Abraham took his wife, Sarai, and all their family, including his nephew Lot and Lot's family. He also took their belongings and herds and flocks.

As Abraham passed through Sichem, a very unusual and astonishing thing happened. Verse 7 says, "And the Lord appeared to Abram and said, 'To your descendants I will give this land'" (NAS, 1977). In other words, God materialized. He renewed His promise to give the land of Israel to Abraham and his family. Abraham built an altar to the Lord there.

The following are some important lessons we learn from this Christophany:

- God has a purpose on earth.
- God has a plan for each person.
- God will go to great lengths to meet people.

God Has a Purpose on Earth

God has a grand design in what He is doing. Before an artist takes a brush to a piece of canvas, he has a picture in his mind. Before a musician ever scribbles a note on a piece of paper, she hears a melody in her heart. Before a sculptor ever picks up a chisel and strikes a blow on a piece of marble, he can already see the statue in his imagination. Just so, God has a plan for this world. He knew exactly what that plan was and how He was going to work it out even before He laid the foundations of this earth or spoke one thing into existence.

The Bible is the record of God working out His providential plan on earth. He takes us from Genesis—the beginning—to Revelation—the end.

God has a plan and a purpose on earth, and He used Abraham and Isaac in bringing these into reality.

God Has a Plan for Each Person

In a sermon titled "Every Life Is a Plan of God," Horace Bushnell said, "Go to God Himself, and ask for the calling of God; for as certainly as he has a plan or calling for you, he will guide you into it."[8]

Does God have an ideal and detailed will and plan for every life? If there is such a plan, how can we know it?

Everywhere in this beautiful world in which we live, there is evidence of a God who is working to a plan. Jesus said:

Are not two sparrows sold for a penny? Yet not one of them will fall to the ground apart from the will of the Father. So, don't be afraid. You are worth more than many sparrows (Matthew 10:29–31).

If our majestic God includes even the insignificant sparrow in His overarching plan and beneficent will, is it unreasonable to conclude that He has an individual plan and purpose for each human life? Each of us is the expression of a unique divine idea, and our purpose in life should be to cooperate with our Father in the outworking of that idea. Each of us is unique because we are made in the image of God.

There is a divine plan for our lives, but we must not expect it to be like an architect's blueprint or like a travel agent's itinerary that is complete with dates, times, and places. We are not robots but people who have been endowed with the awesome power of free choice. Every day, we have to make decisions and choices, with some affecting our whole future. But we have one thing we can be thankful for. Behind the scenes, where we cannot see, there is a divine hand that guides us to where He wants us to be.

The circumstances surrounding our lives are not accidental but are devised by an all-wise and loving Father who knows how best we can glorify Him while at the same time achieving our own highest good.

God doesn't deal with us en masse as much as He does personally and individually. Since each of us is unique, God employs as many methods as there are people. In describing the particularity of the Father's care for His children, Jesus used a striking figure of speech. "Even the very hairs of your head are all numbered" (Matthew 10:30). This gives us assurance that no detail of heredity, peculiarity of temperament, or handicap in environment escapes His compassionate eye. With infinite wisdom and sympathetic understanding, He plans for us in love.

The Lord stated it plainly through the prophet Jeremiah. God said to Jeremiah that when Judah fulfilled the seventy years in captivity, He had a special plan for them.

I know the plan I have for you, plans to prosper you and not to harm you, plans to give you hope and a future. (Jeremiah 29:10–11)

Just as God had a special plan for Abraham, Isaac, and Israel, He has a special plan just for you and just for me.

I may not know God's specific purpose for your life or mine. I may not know what specific goal He has for you or me. I may not know God's grand design as He works in your life and mine. But this I do know: it is to make us more like Jesus. God is not trying to give His people a hard time. Nor is He trying to make us all rich in material goods or trying to make us all happy. But He does want us to be like Jesus in character. If we love Him, we will submit to His control as Abraham did, and He will make all things work together toward His specific purpose. God does have a plan for your life.

God Will Go to Great Lengths to Meet People

Just think about the extreme God went to to reveal Himself to Abraham and Isaac. He sent the preincarnate Son of God so that Abraham and Isaac could meet Him in a real way and understand His love, care, and provision.

And just think of the extreme God went to to reveal Himself to you and me. He came to this earth Himself in His Son, Jesus, to show us what He was like and to do what He wanted to do for us.

There is a palace in Rome with a fresco called the *Aurora*, a work unequalled in that period for nobility of line and poetry of color. It is painted on a very high ceiling. As you stand on the floor and look at it, your neck stiffens, your head grows dizzy, and figures become hazy and indistinct. So, the owner of the palace has placed a mirror near the floor. You can sit down before it and study and admire the wonderful work in comfort.[9]

God has done the same for you and me in Jesus Christ. In Jesus, we get a glimpse of God. Jesus is the exact image of God. In Jesus, God in all His glory becomes visible and understandable to us. In Jesus, we meet God.

CHAPTER 2

CHRIST APPEARS TO HAGAR

Genesis 16

Many Bible scholars believe that our Lord Jesus Himself appeared several times before He came as a baby in Bethlehem. The name for these preincarnate appearances of Jesus is Christophanies. In Genesis 16, Jesus comes and instructs Hagar to return to Sarai and tells her that she will have many descendants. Let's look at the story.

Sarai, Abraham's wife, has not yet had a son as God promised. Sarai is getting old and feeling anxious that she may never have a child. Sarai has an Egyptian maidservant named Hagar. Abraham and Sarai obtained Hagar during their travels to Egypt. Sarai suggests to Abraham that he take Hagar as his wife so she can give Abraham a child. Abraham agrees. Sarai's idea works. Hagar becomes pregnant.

Hagar knew, as the customs of the day dictated, that any child born to her would be adopted by Sarai as her own son. Hagar becomes jealous and begins to act badly toward Sarai. Sarai complains to Abraham about Hagar's disrespectful behavior. Abraham points out that Sarai is Hagar's boss and that she should do whatever she deems necessary to correct the problem. As such, Sarai begins mistreating her servant.

Angry and hurt, Hagar fled Abraham's home and headed back to Egypt, two hundred miles away. During her travel to Egypt, the angel of the

Lord, the preincarnate Christ, found Hagar resting near a spring and asked her, "Where are you coming from and where are you going to?" Hagar explained that her mistress, Sarai, had been mistreating her, so she was returning to her homeland in Egypt. The angel of the Lord instructed Hagar to return to Sarai and continue being her maidservant. All was not lost for Hagar though. The angel promised Hagar that she would have many children, too many too count, and revealed that her soon-to-be-born child would be named Ishmael. The angel pointed out that Ishmael would have a troubled life and would be hostile toward others and that others would be hostile toward him. Ishmael was born when Abraham was eighty-six years old.

John MacArthur, in *The MacArthur Study Bible,* gives this comment on Genesis 16:13: "Recognizing the angel as God and ascribing the new name to him arose from Hagar's astonishment at having been the object of God's gracious attention. The theophany and revelation led her to call him also 'the Living One who sees me.'"[10]

This is the first mention in the Bible of the angel of the Lord. This angel of the Lord is unique in that, throughout scripture, all other angels steadfastly refuse to be worshiped whenever a man or a woman attempts to do so. But that's not the case with the angel of the Lord. His acceptance of worship is an obvious indication that He is deity. I believe that the angel of the Lord is one of the names used in the Old Testament for the second person of the Trinity, Jesus Christ.

What Are We to Learn from This Passage?

1. Sarah could've avoided a lot of trouble if she had just trusted God. God told Sarah that she would give Abraham a son, and eventually she did. But Sarah did not believe God and instead had Hagar give birth to Abraham's son. Since Sarah did not listen to God, it led to many problems between Hagar and Sarah and Hagar's son Ishmael and Sarah's son Isaac. Ishmael, Hagar's son, became the ancestor of the Arabs, who, to this day, are still hostile toward the Jews, Abraham's descendants. The modern strife between Israel

and Palestine is a result of Abraham's and Sarai's decision to not wait for God to fulfill His promise.

2. God-fearing people sometimes try to fulfill God's will in their own ways—and complicate things. But God can even be in their mistakes and use their mistakes to work out His plans. Have you ever made the mistake of taking things into your own hands instead of trusting God?

3. God-fearing people like Abraham and Sarah can still give into jealousy, cruelty, anger, irresponsibility, and pride of class, position, and status. None of this is whitewashed in scripture.

4. God calls people who are foreigners, unbelievers, and of low social status to exalt, bless, and use for His purposes. God, the protector of the downtrodden, delights in helping the despised. Hagar stands alone in the Bible as one who assigns a name to the deity and is the only woman who receives a promise of numerous progenies. Christ appears directly to her in the form of an angel, and she is never the same again.

5. God does not call us to the way of ease or our own way but to go His way, even if it means hardship and suffering. We are not called to pleasure but to the will of God. He calls us to obey even when it is hard—and honors us (and Hagar) when we do so.

6. God always keeps His promises, as Abraham and Sarah would later learn.

7. God still loves us, even when we make mistakes.

CHAPTER 3

CHRIST APPEARS TO JACOB

Genesis 32

Genesis, chapter 32, records an incident in the life of Jacob that beautifully illustrates the positive aspects of change. The truth is that if we are honest, all of us would change something about ourselves.

So Jacob was left alone, and a man wrestled with him till daybreak. When the man saw that he could not overpower him, he touched the socket of Jacob's hip so that his hip was wrenched as he wrestled with the man. (Genesis 32:24–25)

The Bible gives us a view from God's perspective. Someone has said, "He doesn't change us so that He can accept us. He accepts us so that He can change us!"

God loves you just the way you are, but He refuses to leave you that way. If you are going to grow in your walk, you must be willing to allow God to help you to change, to be more and more like Jesus.

I want you to muster up all the imagination you have after a long winter and picture with me a beautiful, sunny summer day with temperatures in the eighties. After church, you're across the street at the park with your little child swinging on the swings and playing in the sandbox. Suddenly you hear the clanging of a bell! You look up, and, lo and behold, there is an old-fashioned ice-cream truck selling ice-cream cones, Fudgsicles, and Creamsicles. You look over at your little one and tell them you'll be right back. You make your way over the thirty feet or so to the truck while keeping that ever-watchful eye on your child. You hand the man the money for the two treats and make your way back to the sandbox, where your little one is happily playing.

But as you bend down to give the delicious treat to your child, you see that their mouth is full of sand. Where you intended to put a delicacy, they have put sand.

The question is, Do you love your child with sand in their mouth? It's a silly question, isn't it? Of course, you love them! Are they any less your child with sand in their mouth? Of course not! But your next step is an obvious one; there is no way you're going to allow them to keep sand in their mouth. You love your child with sand in their mouth, but you refuse to leave them that way. So, you carry them over to the water fountain and wash out their mouth. Why? Because you love them!

God does the same for us. He holds us over the fountain and says, "Spit out the dirt. I've got something better for you," and He cleanses us of the filth, the immorality, the dishonesty, the prejudice, the bitterness, and the greed. We don't enjoy the cleansing; sometimes we even opt for the dirt over the ice cream. "I can eat dirt if I want to!" we pout and proclaim. Which is true, we can. But if we do, the loss is ours. God loves you just the way you are, but He refuses to leave you that way. God has a better offer, and if you are going to grow in your walk, you must be willing to allow God to help you get the dirt out of your mouth so He can give you something so much better.

In the Bible, Jacob was a swindler, a cheat, and a manipulator. But he was changed through a wrestling match with an angel. As God dealt with Jacob in this one-on-one match, Jacob caught a glimpse of what his life could become through change. And change he did.

Jacob Was Changed through a Crisis

What are you wrestling with this week?

What are some of the major changes we face in life?

- loss
- separation
- health
- relationships
- personal growth

How do we deal with these changes? Here are some steps to consider:

o Recognize and understand the change you are going through.
o Accept or reject the change. That is, decide how you are going to let the change affect you.
o Choose your attitude toward this change. We cannot always choose the changes, but we can always choose our attitude toward the change.
o Choose your style of handling the change. Will you use acquiescence, active resistance, or positive acceleration?
o Choose your action. Set out a strategy for dealing with the change.
o Review, evaluate, and adjust as you go along.

Of course, not everyone accepts the need for change gracefully. In a *Peanuts* comic strip I once saw, Lucy is walking along the road with Charlie Brown, who asks, "Lucy, are you going to make any New Year's resolutions?"

Lucy hollers back at him, knocking him off his feet: "What? What for? What's wrong with me now? I like myself the way I am! Why should I change? What in the world is the matter with you, Charlie Brown? I'm all right the way I am! I don't have to improve. How could I improve? How, I ask you? HOW?"

"Everyone thinks of changing the world, but no one thinks of changing himself" (Leo Tolstoy).[11]

Jacob Was Changed through Persistence

Then the man said, "Let me go, for it is daybreak." But Jacob replied, "I will not let you go unless you bless me." (Genesis 32:26)

Have you ever noticed how God often waits to resolve a problem to see if we really mean business? Have you ever looked up to God and said, "God, if You'll get me out of this mess, I promise I'll change"? In the case of Jacob, he was finished being a spiritual sprinter! He was ready to make a commitment to worship the true and living God. He was essentially saying, "I won't cry uncle until You bless me!"

In this day of instant grits, instant coffee, and microwave popcorn, we must remember that spiritual worship does not come without prayer, fasting, and agonizing before God.

Sometimes I think we've lost our ability to persevere before God.

Harold Sherman wrote a book titled *How to Turn Failure into Success.* In it, he gives the following code of persistence:[12]

- o I will never give up so long as I know I am right. I will believe that all things will work out for me if I hang on to the end.
- o I will be courageous and undismayed in the face of odds.
- o I will not permit anyone to intimidate or deter me from my goals.
- o I will fight to overcome all physical handicaps and setbacks.
- o I will try again and again and yet again to accomplish what I desire.
- o I will take new faith and resolution from the knowledge that all successful men and women have had to fight defeat and adversity.
- o I will never surrender to discouragement or despair no matter what seeming obstacles may confront me.

Before Jacob determined to be persistent, I think he had to wrestle with the decision to commit himself to real-life priorities. That can be tough.

Some people make decisions like the family in a story I especially enjoy. It seems the family decided to leave the city and move to the country. They bought a ranch and made plans to raise cattle. They completed the relocation process and set about building their ranch. About six months later, friends came to see them. They wanted to see the ranch and the cattle. The friend said to the owner of the ranch, "What do you call the ranch?"

The owner of the ranch said, "I wanted to call it the Flying W. My wife wanted to name it the Suzie Q. But my oldest son wanted to call it the Bar J, and my youngest son wanted to call it the Lazy Y Ranch."

"So," he said, "what did you name it?"

"Well, we named it the Flying W, Suzie Q, Bar J, Lazy Y Ranch," he said.

"Okay," the friend said, "but where's the cattle?"

The owner said, "Well, we don't have any. None of them survived the branding."[13]

If cattle cannot survive the branding of misplaced priorities, then neither can you. If you can't decide what's important, you're just going to be wounded, beaten up, bruised, battle-scarred, defeated, and discouraged most of the time. When you get your priorities in order, you will cry out, "God, does my life please you?"

When Jacob said, "I will not let You go," he was ready to put God first in his life, even if it cost him everything. Jacob paused to worship God in a time of unparalleled crisis. He was willing to let God change him.

You can change too! It doesn't matter whether you are poor, physically limited, filled with hatred, or manipulative; you don't have to stay bound and oppressed by Satan. You are God's child. He will help you break the chains of sin and overcome the enemy. Satan will be the one who cries uncle.

Jacob Was Changed through Confession

The man asked him, "What is your name?" "Jacob," he answered. (Genesis 32:27)

I've often wondered why the angel asked Jacob his name. The name Jacob means "heel catcher" or "deceiver." It is my personal belief that he answered, "Jacob," in order to confess his sinfulness as a person. If you were to confess your character flaws, what would they be? Tough question? You bet! Right now, there's a big-time wrestling match going on for your soul. When you confess your weaknesses to God, you are on your way to spiritual victory.

Martin Luther, the great leader of the Reformation, was in his study one day, preparing to preach, when he wrote, "Satan came into my study." He said:

While I was seated at my desk studying the Word of God, Satan walked into the room with a huge scroll under his arm. He stopped me in the middle of my studies and said, "Martin Luther, listed on this scroll are all the sins that you've ever committed. Read your sins. Martin Luther, read them!"

Satan held the scroll up by one end and forced me to read all the sins that I had committed in my entire life. Finally, after about an hour of reading all the sinful things that I had done, it seemed as though Hell was going to open up and I was going to fall down into the horrible pit. In desperation, I reached out and took hold of the scroll and unrolling it one more turn, I read, "But the blood of Jesus Christ, God's Son, cleanses us from all sin."[14]

The Bible clearly teaches, "If we confess our sins, he is faithful and just and will forgive us our sins" (1 John 1:9).

Luther knew that, and I hope you do too.

Jacob Was Changed through Worship

Jacob said, "Please tell me your name." But he replied, "Why do you ask my name?" Then he blessed him there. So, Jacob called the place Peniel, saying, "It is because I saw God face to face, and yet my life was spared." (Genesis 32:29–30)

During his time of struggle, Jacob faced God, confessed his weaknesses, and committed his life to Him. That's how he received a new name. His new name was Israel, which means two things: "He who struggles with God" and "Prince of God." The moment Jacob began to worship God, a new name was written down in heaven!

What an incredible gift. That event anticipates the words of the apostle Paul: "Therefore, if anyone is in Christ, he is a new creation; the old has gone, the new has come!" (2 Corinthians 5:17).

Jacob Was Changed through Trust

The sun rose above him as he passed Peniel, and he was limping because of his hip. (Genesis 32:31)

Have you ever wondered why God caused Jacob to walk with a limp the rest of his life? Many scholars believe that his physical disability was a reminder of his need to trust God on a daily basis. Are you like Jacob? Do you need to change? You can, but you cannot do it alone. You must have God's help!

I can attest to the positive changes God has brought in my life through personal challenges, and I am sure you can too. God can do it! Jeremiah said: "Sovereign Lord, you have made the heavens and the earth by your great power and outstretched arm. Nothing is too hard for you" (Jeremiah 32:17).

Here is a simple prayer to pray: "Lord, as I begin this new day, I am resolved to break free of Satan's chains and to change. I am Your expectant child, Holy Spirit. Work in my life to change me for the better, in Jesus's name. Amen!"

CHAPTER 4

CHRIST APPEARS TO MOSES

Exodus 3:1–4:17

Going from the book of Genesis to the book of Exodus, we bridge almost three hundred years, from the death of Joseph to the birth of Moses in about 1552 BC.

Pharaoh had become frightened by Israel because she had grown and expanded as God had promised Abraham. He decided to thin out Israel by killing all the newly born male children. Through the faith and fortitude of Moses's mother and the grace of Pharaoh's daughter, Moses was brought into the palace of Pharaoh, where he was raised.

In the first forty years of Moses's life, he had risen to a position of prominence. Strikingly, Moses identified with his brethren. He abandoned all the luxury and power of the throne of Egypt to stand with his people. However, the brethren misunderstood. Instead of heralding Moses as their deliverer, they turned against him and publicly announced that he was a murderer. With that, Moses fled.

That brings us to our text:

Now Moses was tending the flock of Jethro his father-in-law, the priest of Midian, and he led the flock to the far side of the wilderness and came to Horeb, the mountain of God. There the angel of the Lord appeared to him in flames of fire from within a bush. Moses saw that though the bush was on fire it did not burn up. So Moses thought, "I will go over and see this strange sight—why the bush does not burn up." When the Lord saw that he had gone over to look, God called to him from within the bush, "Moses! Moses!" And Moses said, "Here I am." "Do not come any closer," God said. "Take off your sandals, for the place where you are standing is holy ground." (Exodus 3:1–5)

Moses was out in the desert when he saw a burning bush. To us a burning bush might seem odd, but in the very hot deserts of the Sinai Peninsula, it is not uncommon for a bush to catch fire through spontaneous combustion, and it can be consumed immediately. What was special about this bush was that it didn't burn up. Not only was the bush not consumed, but it spoke with the voice of God Almighty.

Again, we see that phrase "the angel of the Lord," which is identified with Christophanies, the Old Testament appearances of Jesus Christ.

Verse 4 makes it plain that Moses believed this to be God. He uses the word "Lord" (Yahweh) and the word "God" (Elohim).

Verse 5 reminds us of one of the greatest attributes of God. What is it? Holiness. Because Moses was in the presence of God, of Christ, he was on holy ground.

The Lord said, "I have indeed seen the misery of my people in Egypt. I have heard them crying out because of their slave drivers, and I am concerned about their suffering. So I have come down to rescue them from the hand of the Egyptians and to bring them up out of that land into a good and spacious land, a land flowing with milk and honey—the home of the Canaanites, Hittites, Amorites, Perizzites, Hivites and Jebusites. And now the cry of the Israelites has reached me, and I have seen the way the Egyptians are oppressing them. So now, go. I am sending you to Pharaoh to bring my people the Israelites out of Egypt." (Exodus 3:6–10)

God recognized and announced the crisis that faced the nation of Israel. He desired to commission Moses as their deliverer. Things were bad. They had worsened over the past forty years, and God said to Moses, "Therefore, come now, and I will send you to Pharaoh, so that you may bring My people, the sons of Israel, out of Egypt" (Exodus 3:10).

Moses said to God, "Suppose I go to the Israelites and say to them, 'The God of your fathers has sent me to you,' and they ask me, 'What is his name?' Then what shall I tell them?" God said to Moses, "I am who I am. This is what you are to say to the Israelites: 'I am has sent me to you.'" (Exodus 3:13–14)

We might expect Moses to respond like Isaiah did: "Here am I, send me." But no, it is "who am I that I should go to Pharaoh and bring the sons of Israel out of Egypt?"

Excuse 1:
I'm a nobody.
"Who am I?" (Exodus 3:11).

God's Response:
"I will be with you" (Exodus 3:12).
Nobody is a nobody to God!

Excuse 2:
I'm not a theologian.
"What shall I say?" (Exodus 3:13).

God's Response:
"Say to the sons of Israel, I AM has sent me to you"
(Exodus 3:14).

"I AM," that is "I am eternal, unchanging, and the same from the beginning until after the end.

"Moses, when you return tell them you have spoken face to face with the 'I AM,' the Jehovah. Tell them you've been in the presence of the God that doesn't change."

It was the name Abraham knew, the name Jacob knew, and it is the name that you know, for it is used more than seven thousand times in the Old Testament. It was the way Jesus responded to the Pharisee when he said, "Before Abraham was born, I AM" (John 8:58).

When the soldiers came to take Christ in the garden, He said, "Whom do you seek?" They said, "Jesus, the Nazarene." In the Greek language, He uttered one word, the verb "to be"—"I AM." Then the Roman soldiers with all of their might and all of their weapons fell to the ground, because they were in the presence of the living God (John 18:4–6).

"Moses," God said, "you don't have to be a theologian, just tell them that Eternal God sent you."

Excuse 3:

I'm unconvincing.

"What if they will not believe me, or listen to what I say?" (Exodus 4:1).

God's Response:

God gave Moses three signs (Exodus 4:2–9):

- o the rod that would become a serpent
- o the leprous hand,
- o the water that would turn to blood

Excuse 4:

I'm not a preacher.

"I have never been eloquent … I am slow of speech and slow of tongue" (Exodus 4:10).

God's Response:

"I will be with your mouth, and teach you what you are to say" (Exodus 4:12).

Moses still doesn't want to go.

God gets angry (Exodus 4:13).

Moses's unwillingness or lack of faith made God angry. But God's mercy overcame Moses's reluctance, and Aaron was made Moses's spokesman.

Pastor, do you mean God gave a little? Do you mean that God compromised with Moses? Well, that is the way it looks to me. However, God still got His way!

Anyone who thinks they cannot follow the call of God because of personal problems needs to meditate on this passage.

Lessons from This Christophany

1. **God is a holy God.**
   God specifically states through four different prophets that He is holy (Leviticus 11:4, 45; Isaiah 43:3, 15; Ezekiel 39:7; Hosea 11:9). Jesus Christ called God "Holy Father" in John 17:11. Jesus Christ is called holy Himself in numerous places in the Bible, and the other being of the triune God is "Holy" Spirit.

   From the burning bush, God calls out to Moses, "Do not come near; take your sandals off your feet, for the place where you are standing is Holy ground" (Exodus 3:5, ESV). This was a holy place because God was present there in the preincarnate Jesus Christ.

2. **God is concerned about people.**
   God's concern for His people plays out in two different ways. First, God is concerned about being faithful to His promises, and He is concerned about the suffering of His people.

   Exodus 2:24–25 says, "God heard their [the enslaved Israelites] groaning and He remembered His covenant with Abraham, with Isaac and with Jacob. So, God looked on the Israelites and was concerned about them."

   First of all, God is concerned with being faithful to the promises He makes to people. The scripture quoted above says that God "remembered" His covenant with Abraham, Isaac, and Jacob. Even though the Israelites are enslaved by the Egyptians, God had not forgotten the promises He made to them over many generations. He remembers His covenant, or agreement, with Abraham: "I will make you into a great nation" (Genesis 12:2). He remembers that He renewed that covenant with Abraham's son, Isaac: "I am the God of your father, Abraham. Do not be afraid, for I am with you" (Genesis 26:24). And God remembers that, even though Jacob has done many things wrong, He renewed that covenant again with Jacob: "I am the Lord, the God of your father Abraham and the God of Isaac ... I am with you and will watch over you wherever you go" (Genesis 28:13, 15).

God is concerned with being faithful to these promises. As it says in the Psalms, "He is faithful in all He does" (33:4). And as it says in Numbers 23:19, "God is not a human, that He should lie." God is faithful to His promises, and He is concerned about living up to His promises to people. It is helpful for us to remember this in our lives. When we have concerns and worries, God is concerned about being faithful to what He has promised to us.

Secondly, God is concerned with the suffering of His people. After hearing the groans of the Israelites, God calls Moses to be a deliverer for His people. Here are God's words to Moses that reveal His motivations in calling Moses to the job of deliverer: "The Lord said, 'I have indeed seen the misery of my people in Egypt. I have heard them crying out because of their slave drivers, and I am concerned about their suffering. So, I have come down to rescue them'" (Exodus 3:7–8).

God is concerned about their suffering. Many people view God as an impassive, removed deity who has no sense of the pain and suffering we endure in our lives. The picture we see of God here in Exodus is quite different. God is concerned about the suffering of His people.

In the life of Christ, we come face-to-face with God's concern over human suffering. On the one hand, Jesus reaches out to heal and care for people in their suffering. On the other hand, Jesus goes to the cross for the sin and evil of the world, bringing healing to a suffering world: "Surely He took up our pain and bore our suffering" (Isaiah 53:4). God is concerned with the suffering of His people, not only in this Exodus story but also in our daily lives. He hears, and He is concerned about us.

Since we live in a world filled with concerns, it is beneficial to remember that God has concerns as well. He is concerned with being true to His promises to us, and He acts in complete faithfulness with us. God is also concerned with the suffering of His people, and He acts with appropriate care and power to help us.

How has God shown up in your life with His divine concern?

3. **God is angered by unbelief and obstinance.**
    In chapter 4, verses 12–16, Moses's fifth and final statement, notwithstanding the opening supplication, "my Lord, please," was a polite way of bluntly saying, "Choose someone else, not me!" The anger of God toward this overt expression of reluctance was appropriate, yet the Lord still provided another way for His plan to move forward unhindered. Providentially (v. 27), Aaron would meet his brother Moses and positively respond to being the spokesman.

    We anger God with our unbelief and obstinance, but thank God for his mercy, grace, and providence.

CHAPTER 5

CHRIST APPEARS TO BALAAM

Numbers 22:23–25

As the Israelites march to Canaan, they meet and defeat three enemies: the Canaanites, the Amorites, and the Bashanites.

Then the Israelites traveled to the plains of Moab and camped along the Jordan across from Jericho. Now Balak son of Zippor saw all that Israel had done to the Amorites, and Moab was terrified because there were so many people. Indeed, Moab was filled with dread because of the Israelites. The Moabites said to the elders of Midian, "This horde is going to lick up everything around us, as an ox licks up the grass of the field." So Balak son of Zippor, who was king of Moab at that time, sent messengers to summon Balaam son of Beor, who was at Pethor, near the Euphrates River, in his native land. Balak said: "A people has come out of Egypt; they cover the face of the land and have settled next to me. Now come and put a curse on these people, because they are too powerful for me. Perhaps then I will be able to defeat them and drive them out of the land. For I know that whoever you bless is blessed, and whoever you curse is cursed." (Numbers 22:1–6)

The threat of Israel's advance prompts the neighboring pagan nation of Moab under the leadership of Balak to hire the prophet Balaam to bring down a curse upon God's people.

Balaam was a soothsayer or diviner who lived in Pethor. Balaam was not a prophet of Jehovah God. Diviners like Balaam specialized in seeing the future in the entrails (especially livers) of slaughtered animals, in drops of oil on water, in the stars, in clouds.

Balak assumed that Israel must have the blessing of some god on them. Balak summons the most famous supernaturalism in the east to thwart that god's plans.

The name Balaam means devourer of people. His claims of a relationship with Jehovah God were surely false, although the Lord did condescend to speak to Balaam and use him to achieve His own purposes.

The elders of Moab and Midian left, taking with them the fee for divination. When they came to Balaam, they told him what Balak had said. "Spend the night here," Balaam said to them, "and I will report back to you with the answer the Lord gives me." So, the Moabite officials stayed with him. God came to Balaam and asked, "Who are these men with you?" Balaam said to God, "Balak son of Zippor, king of Moab, sent me this message: 'A people that has come out of Egypt covers the face of the land. Now come and put a curse on them for me. Perhaps then I will be able to fight them and drive them away.'" But God said to Balaam, "Do not go with them. You must not put a curse on those people, because they are blessed." The next morning Balaam got up and said to Balak's officials, "Go back to your own country, for the Lord has refused to let me go with you." So the Moabite officials returned to Balak and said, "Balaam refused to come with us." Then Balak sent other officials, more numerous and more distinguished than the first. (Numbers 22:7–15)

God warns Balaam not to do it.

They came to Balaam and said: "This is what Balak son of Zippor says: Do not let anything keep you from coming to me, because I will reward you handsomely and do whatever you say. Come and put a curse on these people for me." But Balaam answered them, "Even if Balak gave me all the silver and gold in his palace, I could not do anything great or small to go beyond the command of the Lord my God. Now spend the night here so that I can find out what else the Lord will tell me." That night God came to Balaam and said, "Since these men have come to summon you, go with them, but do only what I tell you." Balaam got up in the morning, saddled his donkey and went with the Moabite officials. (Numbers 22:16–21)

God says, "Balaam, you can go with them, but you will only say what I tell you to say."

But God was very angry when he went, and the angel of the Lord stood in the road to oppose him. Balaam was riding on his donkey, and his two servants were with him. (Numbers 22:22)

This verse reminds us that God's will was expressed unequivocally in verse 12. Balaam's greed at the prospect of riches (verses 16, 18) caused him to go back to the Lord, hoping for an additional word (verse 19), hoping that God had changed His mind.

The Lord gives Balaam permission to go only in order to teach him, the Moabites, the Israelites, and us the emptiness of pagan divination.

It also provided the Lord opportunity to issue an amazing prophesy of His great plans for Israel.

The Christophany

When the donkey saw the angel of the Lord standing in the road with a drawn sword in his hand, it turned off the road into a field. Balaam beat it to get it back on the road. Then the angel of the Lord stood in a narrow path through the vineyards, with walls on both sides. When the donkey saw the angel of the Lord, it pressed close to the wall, crushing Balaam's foot against it. So, he beat the donkey again. Then the angel of the Lord moved on ahead and stood in a narrow place where there was no room to turn, either to the right or to the left. When the donkey saw the angel of the Lord, it lay down under Balaam, and he was angry and beat it with his staff. Then the Lord opened the donkey's mouth, and it said to Balaam, "What have I done to you to make you beat me these three times?" Balaam answered the donkey, "You have made a fool of me! If only I had a sword in my hand, I would kill you right now." The donkey said to Balaam, "Am I not your own donkey, which you have always ridden, to this day? Have I been in the habit of doing this to you?" "No," he said. (Numbers 22:23–30)

Here is one of the most amusing stories in scripture. Having compared Balaam unfavorably to a witless and obstinate donkey, hired by the fool Balak, the Lord lifted him to the heights of divine revelation and spoke through "this numb-skulled, money-grubbing, heathen seer" a message of messianic deliverance and greatness.

There is no scriptural reason to interpret this passage any other way but literally. If the devil can cause a serpent to speak, as he did in Genesis 3:1, certainly God can do the same with a donkey.

Then the Lord opened Balaam's eyes, and he saw the angel of the Lord standing in the road with his sword drawn. So, he bowed low and fell facedown. The angel of the Lord asked him, "Why have you beaten your donkey these three times? I have come here to oppose you because your path is a reckless one before me. The donkey saw me and turned away from me these three times. If it had not turned away, I would certainly have killed you by now, but I would have spared it." Balaam said to the angel of the Lord, "I have sinned. I did not realize you were standing in the road to oppose me. Now if you are displeased, I will go back." The angel of the Lord said to Balaam, "Go with the men, but speak only what I tell you." So, Balaam went with Balak's officials. When Balak heard that Balaam was coming, he went out to meet him at the Moabite town on the Arnon border, at the edge of his territory. Balak said to Balaam, "Did I not send you an urgent summons? Why didn't you come to me? Am I really not able to reward you?" "Well, I have come to you now," Balaam replied. "But I can't say whatever I please. I must speak only what God puts in my mouth." Then Balaam went with Balak to Kiriath Huzoth. Balak sacrificed cattle and sheep, and gave some to Balaam and the officials who were with him. (Numbers 22:31–40)

Balaam, the "seer" from Mesopotamia, could not see until Jehovah God opened his eyes. Verse 34 says this great prophet did not know until God revealed it to him.

Although this may sound like true repentance on Balaam's part, it is not, as indicated in chapter 25 by his involvement in leading Israel into idolatry.

Verse 40 tells us that Balak sends the diviner Balaam the entrails (livers) of the animals for him to read.

In Numbers 23 and 24 we have Balaam's prophesies.
Instead of a curse, all that could come from Balaam's mouth were blessings upon Israel.

Balaam is promptly fired by Balak.

However, later Balaam does persuade many of the Israelites to marry the pagan women and adopt the immoral ceremonies pertaining to the cults of these heathen tribes.

When Israel overcame the Midianites and Moabites, they slaughtered Balaam along with the leaders of the tribes.

So, the angel of the Lord, Jesus Christ, with sword in hand in front of the donkey, stopped Balaam's devious plan and altered his message. Balaam could only speak the words God gave him, words of blessing to Israel.

Here We Learn

1. **God intervenes, sometimes dramatically, in the affairs of humankind.**
   Divine intervention is, simply put, God intervening in the affairs of the world. Divine intervention can be God causing something to happen or God preventing something from happening.

Biblically speaking, God definitely intervenes in the affairs of the world. We see His intervention from Genesis through Revelation. God is sovereign (Psalm 93:1, 95:3; Jeremiah 23:20; Romans 9). Nothing happens that God does not ordain, cause, or allow. We are constantly surrounded by divine intervention, even when we are ignorant of it or blind to it. We will never know all of the times and all of the ways God intervenes in our lives. Divine intervention can come in the form of a miracle, such as a healing or supernatural sign. Divine intervention can also come in the form of a seemingly random event that directs us in the way God wants us to go.

2. **God can take the evil interest of ignorant prophets and turn them for His glory.**

   There is an important distinction to be made between God *controlling* evil and God *creating* evil. God is not the author of sin, but He can use sinful people to attain an objective. Romans 8:28 says, "For those who love God all things work together for good, for those who are called according to his purpose." "All things" includes both good and bad things. God can use struggles, heartbreaks, and tragedies in ways to bring about His glory and our good. Such events, even though we don't understand the reason for them, are part of His perfect, divine plan. If God could not control evil, He would not be God. His sovereignty demands that He be in control of everything, even "evil" prophets like Balaam and his donkey.

3. **God's plan is a blessing for His people.**

   Every Christian knows that God has a plan. He has plans for each person, each nation, and for the entire world. That does not mean, however, that Christians do not sometimes look at the world around them and struggle to find the method to the madness. They may even struggle to remember that there is a plan at all. In those moments, scripture can be a good way for Christians to remind themselves that God has a plan.

Jeremiah 29:11 reminds Christians that God's plan is to bless His people. Jeremiah 29 was written to the Jews in exile, a group of people who were seeing only the low points of God's plan. Jeremiah reminded them, however, that God is always watching over His people. The verse reads, "'For I know the plans I have for you,' declares the Lord, 'plans to prosper you and not to harm you, plans to give you hope and a future.'" That is a good promise to memorize!

CHAPTER 6

CHRIST APPEARS TO JOSHUA
Joshua 5:1–15

Israel had experienced a great miracle, the enemy was frightened, and God was at work. Now was the time for action. But God told His people to wait. Why? So that He might prepare them for the conquest of the land. What must be done before the conquest can begin?

1. **Dealing with the Past (Verses 1–9)**

After triumphantly crossing the Jordan River, the nation had to pause at Gilgal while the men submitted to the painful surgery of circumcision. Why did God command this?

A. **To Restore Their Covenant Relationship (Verses 2–7)**
Israel had privilege given to no other nation on earth. God gave His covenant to Abraham when He called him out of Ur of the Chaldees, and He sealed that covenant with a sacrifice. God gave circumcision as the sign of the covenant to Abraham and his descendants.

Through the ritual of circumcision, the Jews became a "marked people" because they belonged to the true and living God. This meant they were under obligation to obey Him. The mark of the covenant reminded them that their bodies belonged to the Lord and were not to be used for sinful purposes.

Israel was surrounded by nations that worshiped idols and included in their worship rituals that were sensual and degrading. The mark of the covenant reminded the Jews that they were a special people, a separated people, a holy nation, and that they were to maintain purity in their marriages, their society, and their worship of God.

All of the adult males who left Egypt with Moses for the Promised Land had experienced circumcision. But all of these had died during the forty years in the wilderness because of their sin. The Jews had not practiced circumcision in the wilderness. Therefore, it was now necessary, as the covenant was being renewed, for all the males to be circumcised.

According to Deuteronomy 10:16, the physical operation was meant to be a symbol of a spiritual operation on the heart.

Circumcision symbolized putting off what belonged to the sinful flesh and devoting the heart wholeheartedly to God.

B. **To Test Their Faith (Verse 8)**
"And after the whole nation had been circumcised, they remained where they were in camp until they were healed."

C. **To Remove Their Reproach (Verse 9)**
"Then the Lord said to Joshua, 'Today I have rolled away the reproach of Egypt from you.' So, the place has been called Gilgal to this day."

Their reproach was the shame for having disobeyed God and therefore having wandered in the wilderness for forty years.

2. **Trusting for the Present (Verses 10–12)**

   The Passover was first celebrated forty years earlier on the night of their deliverance from Egypt. The Passover was to be a reminder that they were a redeemed people, set free by the blood of the lamb.

   Now as they began the conquest of the Promised Land, they needed to remember who redeemed them and how He had provided for their every need in the past. This would remind them that they could also count on Him in the present.

   Of course, the death of Jesus Christ is typified in the slaying of the Passover lamb.

   While in the wilderness, God provided miraculously for His people with manna from heaven.

   Now the nation stopped eating manna and started eating food that God naturally provided. There is a place for the miraculous, but God never wastes miracles.

   One thing was sure. Just as God had provided for their needs in the wilderness, they could count on Him to provide for their needs in the present. We can too!

3. **Submitting for the Future (Verses 13–15)**

   Joshua stole out of camp in the darkness to view Jericho for himself and seek God's guidance. The Hebrew word that tells us that Joshua was "by Jericho" expresses the idea of immediate proximity. He was very close, perhaps close enough to feel the oppression of the city described as "walled to heaven."

   There Joshua remained in the night brooding … meditating. … patrolling, his eyes fixed to the ground when he detected some movement in the periphery of his vision and raised his eyes. What he saw set his heart racing and adrenalin pumping. For there stood a warrior in full battle dress, his sword drawn and gleaming in the moon's light.

A less courageous man would have bolted. But not Joshua. His hand no doubt upon his own sword, he strode forward, calling out to the figure, "Are you for us or for our adversaries? Which side are you on … ours or the enemies? Because if you are from Jericho, then it will be steel against steel!" Joshua was no armchair general.

- **First, there is revelation (verses 13-14a).**

I believe that this "captain of the host of the Lord" was a Christophany, an Old Testament appearance, a preincarnate appearance of Jesus Christ.

Why do I believe this? Well, first Joshua was told to take off his shoes, and this is the very same command given to Moses at the burning bush.

Second, He is identified as the "Lord." And third, Joshua knew not only that He was of God but also that he was God. For he would not have worshipped Him had he not recognized Him as God in the flesh.

As Joshua faced the battles ahead, he needed this revelation of God as the "Lord of Host." He needed to be assured of the Lord's presence and power with Him and His people.

The awareness of God's presence and power with us makes all the difference in the world.

The first chapter of Revelation tells us that Christ walks among His churches. He walks down the aisles of our church today. He stands on the platform before you each Sunday. He walks with us as we leave this place and go out to conquer new territory for Him each week.

As individuals, we will face difficulties this coming year. As a church, as we accept the challenge to continue to build for Him, we will be faced with challenges and difficulties. Isn't it great to know that He will be with us? How edifying, how up-building should that sense of God's presence be to us.

- **Second, there is realization—the realization that He will fight for us (verse 14).**

What do we learn from this? Just this: "If God be for us who can be against us" (Romans 8:31).

We also learn that we do not fight with conventional weapons.

Second Corinthians 10:3–4 reminds us, "For though we live in the world, we do not wage war as the world does. The weapons we fight with are not the weapons of the world. On the contrary, they have divine power to demolish strongholds."

- **Third, there is worship (verses 14b—15).**

The moonlight revealed Joshua doing three things:

o He hit the sand immediately with no hesitation—instant submission.
o He verbalized his commitment: "What has my Lord to say to His servant?" … "Lord, you say it, I'll do it."
o He responded immediately to the command to remove his sandals in holy reverence.

The lesson of the moonlight is clear for all of us: if we are to fight the battles of life successfully, we must be totally, worshipfully submitted. Worshipful submission and commitment can turn us into modern-day Joshuas.

4. **Fourth, There Is Guidance from God (Joshua 6:2–5)**
   One final element is necessary for meeting the challenges that await us, and that is receiving divine directions from the Lord. Human direction can have its drawbacks.

A story was told in *Sunshine* magazine about a family who had moved into a new neighborhood.

One morning, they overslept, and Jimmy, the youngest, missed his ride on the school bus. His father offered to drive him to school, although he didn't know where the school was located.

So, they started out, with Jimmy giving the directions. Going a few blocks, they made a left turn, then a right turn. As they continued along the route, they made several other turns.

About twenty-five minutes later, they finally arrived at their destination. Much to the father's amazement, the school was quite close to home. "Jimmy," the father said, "how come you took me so far around?"

His son replied quiet apologetically, "I'm sorry, Dad. That's how our bus goes! It's the only way I know."[15]

Divine direction never fails, though at times it may not make sense to human logic. Jesus, the "captain of the hosts," was very clear in the directions He gave to Joshua.

Then the Lord said to Joshua, "See, I have delivered Jericho into your hands, along with its king and its fighting men. March around the city once with all the armed men. Do this for six days. Have seven priests carry trumpets of rams' horns in front of the ark. On the seventh day, march around the city seven times, with the priests blowing the trumpets. When you hear them sound a long blast on the trumpets, have the whole army give a loud shout; then the wall of the city will collapse and the army will go up, everyone straight in." (Joshua 6:2–5)

These plans thoroughly contradicted human wisdom. Common-sense warfare required intelligent regimentation of the troops and specialization. They needed battering rams, scaling equipment, and other engines of war. Marching around the city could well leave them open to a murderous attack. And the imposed silence was absurd, especially when the marching warriors had to listen to the jeers of Jericho's Amorites. The plans God gave Joshua didn't make sense at all according to human logic.

But Joshua lived by faith. Hebrews 11:30 says, "By faith the walls of Jericho fell down, after they had been encircled seven days" (CSB).

It took faith to follow God's directions for spiritual warfare. It takes faith to war "according to the flesh."

Following God's direction always takes faith, and it always pays off.

None of us will ever experience the kinds of pressure Joshua knew that night as he meditated under the ramparts of Jericho, but we do face situations, personal Jerichos, that are more than we can handle. And Joshua's experience tells us what is spiritually necessary for the challenge:

- We must have a revelation of God's presence with us.
- We must have a realization that God will fight for us.
- We must have a submissive worship.
- We must follow God's directions completely, even if it means being thought foolish.

Rest in His presence. Believe it. See His sword drawn in our behalf. Fall before Him in submissive worship and do what He says. On the seventh day (the day of God's choice), the walls will come tumbling down.

CHAPTER 7

CHRIST APPEARS TO GIDEON
Judges 6:1–24

Here we see how God works in the lives of His people to bring restoration.

First, notice this:

1. **Rebellion (verse 1a)**
    "The Israelites did evil in the eyes of the Lord."

    Through the book of Judges and all the historical books, this is the regular phrase for falling into idolatry. It occurs seven times in Judges and is descriptive of the seven apostasies of Israel, which drew down upon them the seven servitudes under the following:

    (1) Chushan-Rishathaim
    (2) Eglon
    (3) Jabin
    (4) Midian
    (5) the tyranny of Abimelech
    (6) the Ammonites
    (7) the Philistines

Second, notice this:

2. **Retribution (verses 1b–6a)**
   "And for seven years the Lord gave them into the hands of Midianites."

The wandering herdsmen from east of the Red Sea had been dealt a severe blow in Moses's time and still resented the Israelites. God punished His people's sin by giving them over to the Midianites. They became the worst scourge yet to afflict Israel.

Because the power of Midian was so oppressive, the Israelites prepared shelters for themselves in mountain clefts, caves, and strongholds (v. 2).

Whenever the Israelites planted their crops, the Midianites, Amalekites, and other eastern peoples invaded the country (v. 3).

They camped on the land and ruined the crops all the way to Gaza and did not spare a living thing for Israel, neither sheep nor cattle nor donkeys (v. 4).

They came up with their livestock and their tents like swarms of locusts. It was impossible to count them or their camels; they invaded the land to ravage it (v. 5).

Midian so impoverished the Israelites that they cried out to the Lord for help (v. 6).

The strategy of the Midianites was clever. They did not seek to occupy the land but simply waited until the harvest was ready. Then they swept in and overwhelmed the land, stripping it bare like a plague of locusts would do.

A major factor in their success was a new military weapon—the camel, used here for the first time in an organized raid. These creatures possessed an endurance and speed that enabled them to travel as far as one hundred miles a day without food or water, carrying heavy loads on their backs.

No wonder the frightened Israelites were rendered helpless and were forced to leave hearth and home and flee for their lives to caves and caverns in the mountains.

Harvest after harvest, they repeated their raids. It appeared that nothing could stop them. Israel was reduced to a state of national disaster. At last they came to their senses and cried out to the Lord.

Then there was this:

3. **Repentance (verses 6b–10)**

    Midian so impoverished the Israelites that they cried out to the Lord for help. When the Israelites cried out to the Lord because of Midian, he sent them a prophet, who said, "This is what the Lord, the God of Israel, says: I brought you up out of Egypt, out of the land of slavery. I rescued you from the hand of the Egyptians. And I delivered you from the hand of all your oppressors; I drove them out before you and gave you their land. I said to you, 'I am the Lord your God; do not worship the gods of the Amorites, in whose land you live.' But you have not listened to me."

God did not immediately send a deliverer as He did before. The people of Israel appeared to be turning to the Lord as a last resort, pleading for escape from their misery without giving attention to the reason for their misfortune.

So, the Lord sent a prophet to deliver His message. The message reminded the hearers of God's work in redeeming Israel out of Egypt and rebuked them for having feared the gods of the Amorites rather than obeying the one true God of the Israelites.

The people needed to recognize the nature of their sin and repent of it. God's message was that repentance is necessary before restoration.

From what follows in the text, the ministry of the prophet seems to have accomplished its purpose.

Then there was this:

4. **Restoration (verses 11–24)**

The Christophany, verses 11–16:

> The angel of the Lord came and sat down under the oak in Ophrah that belonged to Joash the Abiezrite, where his son Gideon was threshing wheat in a winepress to keep it from the Midianites. When the angel of the Lord appeared to Gideon, he said, "The Lord is with you, mighty warrior." "Pardon me, my lord," Gideon replied, "but if the Lord is with us, why has all this happened to us? Where are all his wonders that our ancestors told us about when they said, 'Did not the Lord bring us up out of Egypt?' But now the Lord has abandoned us and given us into the hand of Midian." The Lord turned to him and said, "Go in the strength you have and save Israel out of Midian's hand. Am I not sending you?" "Pardon me, my lord," Gideon replied, "but how can I save Israel? My clan is the weakest in Manasseh, and I am the least in my family." The Lord answered, "I will be with you, and you will strike down all the Midianites, leaving none alive."

Note that the one who speaks with Gideon is called the "Angel of the Lord" in verses 11 and 12 but "the Lord" in verses 14 and 16.

The phrase "angel of the Lord" and "the Lord" are used synonymously. This angel was none other than Jesus Christ in the flesh, a preincarnate appearance of Christ in the Old Testament.

In verses 17–22, Gideon asks for a sign:

Gideon replied, "If now I have found favor in your eyes, give me a sign that it is really you talking to me. Please do not go away until I come back and bring my offering and set it before you." And the Lord said, "I will wait until you return." Gideon went inside, prepared a young goat, and from an ephah of flour he made bread without yeast. Putting the meat in a basket and its broth in a pot, he brought them out and offered them to him under the oak. The angel of God said to him, "Take the meat and the unleavened bread, place them on this rock, and pour out the broth." And Gideon did so. Then the angel of the Lord touched the meat and the unleavened bread with the tip of the staff that was in his hand. Fire flared from the rock, consuming the meat and the bread. And the angel of the Lord disappeared. When Gideon realized that it was the angel of the Lord, he exclaimed, "Alas, Sovereign Lord! I have seen the angel of the Lord face to face!"

In verses 23–24, Gideon goes to work:

But the Lord said to him, "Peace! Do not be afraid. You are not going to die." So Gideon built an altar to the Lord there and called it The Lord Is Peace. To this day it stands in Ophrah of the Abiezrites.

Lessons from This Christophany

- **God sees us as we can be, not as we are.**

God sees us as we are, loves us as we are, and accepts us as we are. But by His grace, He does not leave us as we are. Just as God saw Gideon's potential, He sees yours and mine too.

When Jesse was passing all of his sons before the Lord so that God would choose a king for Israel from among them, Samuel was certain that one of them would be the next king, for Jesse's oldest sons were tall, strong, and handsome. So, Samuel said, "'Surely the Lord's anointed is before him.' But the Lord said to Samuel, 'Do not look on his appearance or on the height of his stature, because I have rejected him. For the Lord sees not as man sees: man looks on the outward appearance, but the Lord looks on the heart'" (1 Samuel 16:6–7). God's choice was the last one they would have ever considered, but David was a man after God's own heart (Acts 13:22), especially knowing that God can see into the heart and know what's there. We can only see the face, but God sees the heart.

- **God is still there when we feel abandoned.**

Gideon was hiding out. He felt abandoned by God. But that was not the case.

Remember Job? If anyone in history ever walked through a season of darkness and feelings of abandonment, it was Job. Common sense tells us that we can learn from others who have experienced what we're going through, especially those who have come through to the other side. It's not only common sense, but in the New Testament, Paul tells us that it is God who comforts us in all our troubles, so that we can comfort those in any trouble with the comfort we ourselves receive from God" (2 Corinthians 1:4).

Remember, God is still there, even if you feel abandoned.

- **God delivers us from overwhelming odds**

(Judges 7).

In Judges 7, we read that to prevent an attitude of self-sufficiency among the soldiers, God told Gideon to limit the number of men attacking the enemy. From tens of thousands in the army, God eventually reduced the final attacking party to just three hundred men. In this way, neither Gideon nor his men could take the credit away from God.

Knowing that Gideon needed assurance, especially when God had reduced the size of his army, God arranged for him and his servant Purah to slip into the enemy's camp to overhear a conversation that would give him courage. God put a dream into the enemy and also gave them an interpretation to encourage Gideon.

Finally, like when Joshua surrounded Jericho, Gideon and his three hundred men surrounded the Midianite camp. All they did was sound the trumpet and break the jars. The commotion created panic in the enemy camp, and the confusion caused them to kill one another. Gideon and his men simply watched God delivering the enemy to Israel.

You can count on God delivering you, too, even against overwhelming odds.

CHAPTER 8

CHRIST APPEARS TO MANOAH'S WIFE

Judges 13

The story of Samson is a story of a great opportunity and a dismal failure. The puzzle of Samson's life is this: while he was so richly endowed with potential for blessing and victory, he failed to live up to his potential and ended his life in disgrace.

Look at what the *Expositors Bible Commentary* says about Samson:

In raw, giant strength and wild daring Samson stands alone. He was a man of wit but not of wisdom. He was great, but could have been outstanding. As with so many men … his strength was his weakness … there was strictness, yet laxity. Many a man like Samson has loved some woman "in the valley of Sorek!" The entire world is a valley of Sorek to weak men, and at every turn, he needs Someone higher than himself to guard and guide him. Like this Judge of Israel, his unbridled passion and overwhelming desires made him a child in morals, though full grown in mind and muscles.[16]

Samson was to be a leader in Israel and God's instrument to deliver His people, but, unfortunately, his walk with God was erratic and his contacts with God infrequent.

Let's look at Samson's beginnings.

1. **The Rebellion**
   "Again the Israelites did evil in the eyes of the Lord" (verse 1a).

   Much has happened in the lives of God's people after their conquest of Canaan. They have been on a roller coaster in terms of their relationship with God. They do evil in the sight of the Lord. God punishes them by delivering them into the hands of an enemy. They beg for a deliverer, and God sends one in the form of a judge.

   Not much has changed, as we will see here in Judges 13. Verse 1 reminds us, "Again the Israelites did evil in the eyes of the Lord, so that the Lord gave them into the hands of the Philistines forty years." The Philistines had been enemies of God's people for some time and would continue to be for years to come. They were not conquered and destroyed during the conquest of Canaan by Joshua (cf. Joshua 3:1–2). After Joshua's death, we see the tribes continuing to conquer Canaan; however, they didn't completely destroy these people. Rather, they allowed them to dwell among them (cf. Judges 1). The Philistines, thus, were for testing Israel (Judges 3:1–4).

2. **The Retribution**
   "So the Lord delivered them into the hands of the Philistines for forty years" (verse 1b).

   As punishment for their idolatry, the Lord allowed the Philistines to oppress Israel for forty years. This is the longest oppression Israel experienced. The career of Samson is set at this time.

   Something is missing here in this passage that was there in the other cycles. Always before, in their desperation, the people repented and cried out to God for a deliverer.

The rule of the Philistines at this time was not cruel, so the Israelites accepted their rule with apathy and docility and even came to resent Samson's exploits to deliver them.

So, the Lord did not send a national deliverer but raised up Samson, who waged a one-man war against the Philistines.

We must judge Samson harshly because, despite his privileges and his calling, his life revolved around self-indulgence.

We are left to wonder what he might have achieved.

3. The Revelation (Judges 13:2–20)

- **Christophany 1**

A certain man of Zorah, named Manoah, from the clan of the Danites, had a wife who was childless, unable to give birth. The angel of the Lord appeared to her and said, "You are barren and childless, but you are going to become pregnant and give birth to a son. Now see to it that you drink no wine or other fermented drink and that you do not eat anything unclean. You will become pregnant and have a son whose head is never to be touched by a razor because the boy is to be a Nazirite, dedicated to God from the womb. He will take the lead in delivering Israel from the hands of the Philistines." Then the woman went to her husband and told him, "A man of God came to me. He looked like an angel of God, very awesome. I didn't ask him where he came from, and he didn't tell me his name. But he said to me, 'You will become pregnant and have a son. Now then, drink no wine or other fermented drink and do not eat anything unclean, because the boy will be a Nazirite of God from the womb until the day of his death.'" Then Manoah prayed to the Lord: "Pardon your servant, Lord. I beg you to let the man of God you sent to us come again to teach us how to bring up the boy who is to be born." (Verses 2–8)

Manoah and family were Danites (from the tribe of Dan) living in Zorah—a city of Dan that was about thirteen miles west of Jerusalem, on the border of Judah. Manoah's wife was barren and had borne no children. We are not told if she couldn't have children or if they were just waiting. It wasn't customary to put off childbirth, so I would suspect she couldn't have children. Her barren and childless condition was considered a tragedy in Israel, because the family line could not continue.

Her intense frustration, however, was put to an end by two appearances of the "angel of the Lord." This is a Christophany, a preincarnate appearance of Jesus Christ. Manoah's wife obviously has been selected by God to carry out His will.

The angel, this messenger Jesus, brings an astounding message to her, an answer to her deep longings and prolonged prayers.

She was going to have a son, and he was to be set apart as a Nazarite. He would be obligated to keep the law of the Nazarite vow found in Numbers 6:1–8. The Nazarite vow was undertaken by a man or a woman voluntarily in order to fulfill some specific service to God.

The word "Nazarite" means separated or consecrated.[17] The heavenly messenger instructed that the child was to demonstrate his separation to the Lord by keeping the three requirements of the Nazarite vow:

o He was to abstain from the fruit of the vine, indicating his dedication to live a simple life (v. 4).
o He was to refrain from cutting his hair as a public sign of his vow to God (v. 5).
o He was to avoid contact with a dead body, an act that would disqualify him for tabernacle worship (Numbers 6:6).

Samson was to avoid anything that marred his fellowship with God. These outward actions would be meaningless unless they truly represented an inner dedication of life.

The angel made it clear that Samson was to be a Nazarite all of his life. He was to be a man marked by dedication to God. Even his mother was restricted from drinking strong drink or eating unclean foods while she was carrying the child, lest he be contaminated with that which would violate the Nazarite vow.

Here in verse 5, it is clear that God meant for Samson to deliver His people from the yoke of the Philistines.

But because of Samson's failure to live up to his call, it would be left to others such as Samuel, Saul, and David to break the yoke of the Philistines.

- **Christophany 2 (Judges 13:9–20)**

  Verse 20 tells us that as the flame blazed up from the altar toward heaven, the angel of the Lord ascended in the flame. Seeing this, Manoah and his wife fell with their faces to the ground.

  This second appearance of the angel came in answer to the prayer of Manoah in verse 8.

  Manoah believed his wife's report and asked the Lord, "Teach us what to do for the boy who is to be born."

  God heard Manoah, and the angel of God came again to the woman while she was out in the field; but her husband Manoah was not with her. The woman hurried to tell her husband, "He's here! The man who appeared to me the other day!" Manoah got up and followed his wife. When he came to the man, he said, "Are you the man who talked to my wife?" "I am," he said. So Manoah asked him,

"When your words are fulfilled, what is to be the rule that governs the boy's life and work?" (Verses 9–12)

What shall be the boy's mode of life and vocation?

"The angel of the Lord answered, 'Your wife must do all that I have told her'" (verse 13).

The angel didn't answer Manoah's question but cautioned Manoah that his wife was to be careful to observe all the restrictions he had previously imposed.

"She must not eat anything that comes from the grapevine, nor drink any wine or other fermented drink nor eat anything unclean. She must do everything I have commanded her" (verse 14).

He should be content with what God revealed.

Manoah was much like God's people today. We would like to know all the steps ahead of us before beginning with the first step, rather than trusting God to reveal the steps in the proper time.

We must note that Manoah and his wife desperately wanted to fulfill their parental responsibility and raise their child to honor and serve God. They were concerned about doing their best as godly parents for Samson.

Manoah said to the angel of the Lord, "We would like you to stay until we prepare a young goat for you." The angel of the Lord replied, "Even though you detain me, I will not eat any of your food. But if you prepare a burnt offering, offer it to the Lord." (Manoah did not realize that it was the angel of the Lord.) Then Manoah inquired of the angel of the Lord, "What is your name, so that we may honor you when your word comes true?" (verses 15–17).

Manoah was still not aware of the identity of the visitor who brought this news, so the angel did three things to reveal his identity:

"He replied, 'Why do you ask my name? It is beyond understanding'" (v. 18).

My name is a "wonderful name" (secret).

Then Manoah took a young goat, together with the grain offering, and sacrificed it on a rock to the Lord. And the Lord did an amazing thing while Manoah and his wife watched: the Lord performed wonders in the presence of Manoah and his wife (v. 19).

As the flame blazed up from the altar toward heaven, the angel of the Lord ascended in the flame. Seeing this, Manoah and his wife fell with their faces to the ground (v. 20).

4. **The Realization**
   When the angel of the Lord did not show himself again to Manoah and his wife, Manoah realized that it was the angel of the Lord. "We are doomed to die!" he said to his wife. "We have seen God!" But his wife answered, "If the Lord had meant to kill us, he would not have accepted a burnt offering and grain offering from our hands, nor shown us all these things or now told us this." (Verses 21–23)

   o   They realized they had seen God.
   o   They realized that the birth of their son had just been announced by God's preincarnate Son, the messenger of the Lord.

What about us today? Should we stand ready to serve God? Most definitely! Of course, we shouldn't expect a visit from an angel with a similar message, but we have opportunities daily to serve God in many ways. Paul told the Ephesians to, "make the most of every opportunity" (Eph. 5:16). How are some ways we stand ready to serve God?

- We have to be strong spiritually. Do you think God opens as many doors of opportunity for a spiritually weak person?

- We have to put God first in our lives. Jesus told us to "seek ye first the kingdom of God (Matt. 6:33, KJV). Paul admonishes us in that "whatever you do in word or deed, do all in the name of the Lord Jesus" (Col. 3:17). How many times have people missed opportunities to serve God by allowing other worldly things to get in the way?

- We have to be well equipped. Manoah's wife was equipped with the spiritual knowledge she needed to carry out her task. What do I mean by that? Notice verse 5: "the boy shall be a Nazirite to God from the womb." Had Manoah's wife not been a spiritual woman, well versed in God's law, she wouldn't have had the knowledge to carry out this vow. She might not even know what it was. The particulars regarding this vow are outlined in Numbers 6:1–21. It's important to note that this vow started from the womb, meaning she had to live by it herself. What's the point for us today? How can we carry out God's will if we are not students of His Word? We must be active students of God's Word, standing ready to serve.

POSTSCRIPT

Just as Christ's existence didn't begin with His birth in Bethlehem, neither did it end with His earthly death in Jerusalem. After three days, He rose from the grave, ascended to heaven, and sat down at the right hand of God the Father, where He lives to intercede for us (Mark 16:19; Hebrews 1:3, 7:25). God's presence now lives in each believer through the Holy Spirit. What a joy to know that the Holy Spirit of God is always with us (John 14:16–17, 16:7–14).

The God who has appeared throughout all of history, whose work we see in creation and whose sacrifice assured our salvation, will appear again one day before our eyes. In that day, the whole world will respond in worship and praise to Him (Philippians 2:9–11). What a day that will be!

Chapter 1 Outline
Christ Appears to Abraham
Genesis 12:1–9

1. Abraham is described as the following:
    *   the friend of God (2 Chronicles 20:7)
    *   a man of faith and prayer (Genesis 15:6, 18:23–33).
    *   a man determined to be obedient to the Lord, whatever the cost (Genesis 22:1–18; Hebrews 11:8–10)

2. God's promise to Abraham was fulfilled:
    *   in Abraham's temporal blessings (Genesis 13:2; 24:35)
    *   in Abraham's spiritual blessings (Genesis 21:22)
    *   in Abraham's fame (Genesis 23:6; Isaiah 41:8)

3. God's promise was fulfilled imminently in the birth of his son Isaac and eternally through the coming of Jesus Christ from Abraham's seed (Galatians 3:8,16).

4. In verse 7, we see the Christophany. There are three important lessons we learn from this Christophany:
    *   God has a purpose on earth.
    *   God has a plan for each person.
    *   God will go to great lengths to meet a person.

Chapter 2 Outline
Christ Appears to Hagar
Genesis 16

Many Bible scholars believe that our Lord Jesus Himself appeared several times before He came as a baby in Bethlehem. The name for these preincarnate appearances of Jesus is Christophanies.

Here in Genesis 16, Jesus comes and instructs Hagar to return to Sarah and told her that she would have many descendants.

What are we to learn from this passage?

1. Sarah could've avoided a lot of trouble if she had just trusted God.
2. God-fearing people sometimes try to fulfill God's will in their own ways—and complicate things. But God can even be in their mistakes and use their mistakes to work out his plans. Have you ever made the mistake of taking things into your own hands instead of trusting God?
3. God-fearing people like Abraham and Sarah can still give into jealousy, cruelty, anger, irresponsibility, and pride of class, position, and status. None of this is whitewashed in scripture.
4. God calls people who are foreigners, unbelievers, and of low social status to exalt, bless, and use for His purposes. God, the protector of the downtrodden, delights in helping the despised.
5. God calls us not to ease or our own way but to go His way, even if it means hardship and suffering. We are called not to pleasure but to the will of God. He calls us to obey even when it is hard—and honors us (and Hagar) when we do so.
6. God always keeps His promises, as Abraham and Sarah later learn.
7. God still loves us, even when we make mistakes.

Chapter 3 Outline
Christ Appears to Jacob
Genesis 32

In the Bible, Jacob was a swindler, a cheat, and a manipulator. But he was changed through a wrestling match with an angel. As God dealt with Jacob in this one-on-one match, Jacob caught a glimpse of what his life could become through change. And change he did.

- Jacob was changed through a crisis.

- Jacob was changed through persistence.
  Genesis 32:26: "Then the man said, 'Let me go, for it is daybreak.' But Jacob replied, 'I will not let you go unless you bless me.'"

- Jacob was changed through confession.
  Genesis 32:27: "The man asked him, 'What is your name?' 'Jacob,' he answered."

- Jacob was changed through worship.
  Genesis 32:29–30:

  Jacob said, "Please tell me your name." But he replied, "Why do you ask my name?" Then he blessed him there. So, Jacob called the place Peniel, saying, "It is because I saw God face to face, and yet my life was spared."

- Jacob was changed through trust.
  Genesis 32:31: "The sun rose above him as he passed Peniel, and he was limping because of his hip."

Have you ever wondered why God caused Jacob to walk with a limp the rest of his life? Many scholars believe that his physical disability was a reminder of his need to trust God on a daily basis. Are you like Jacob? Do you need to change? You can, but you cannot do it alone. You must have God's help.

Chapter 4 Outline
Christ Appears to Moses
Exodus 3:1–4:17

Jesus appeared to Moses in the burning bush with the command to go to Egypt and proclaim deliverance for Israel.

Moses used four excuses that are still around today:

1. Excuse: Exodus 3:11
   God's response: Exodus 3:12

2. Excuse: Exodus 3:13
   God's response: Exodus 3:14

3. Excuse: Exodus 4:1
   God's response: Exodus 4:2–9

4. Excuse: Exodus 4:10
   God's response: Exodus 4:12

Lessons from This Christophany

- God is a holy God (Exodus 3:5).
- God is concerned for His people (Exodus 3:7–8).
- The Lord is angered by unbelief and obstinance (Exodus 4:14).

Chapter 5 Outline
Christ Appears to Balaam
Numbers 22:23–25

The prophet Balaam is hired by Balak, King of Moab, to put a curse on the people of Israel. On his way to do so, the "angel of the Lord," the preincarnate Christ, appears and blocks Balaam's path.

The Lord Jesus tells Balaam not to curse Israel but to say only what He says to say. Instead of a curse, all that could come from Balaam's mouth were blessings for Israel.

Lessons We Learn from This Christophany:

1. God intervenes, sometimes dramatically, in the affairs of humankind.
2. God can take the evil interests of ignorant prophets and turn them for His glory.
3. God's plan is a blessing for His people.

Chapter 6 Outline
Christ Appears to Joshua
Joshua 5:1–15

Israel had experienced a great miracle, the enemy was frightened, and God was at work. Now was the time for action. But God told His people to wait. Why? So that He might prepare them for the conquest of the land. What must be done before the conquest can begin?

1. They must deal with the past. Why deal with the past?
   • to restore their covenant relationship (verses 2–7)
   • to test their faith (verse 8)
   • to remove their reproach (verse 9)

2. They must trust for the present (verses 10–12).

3. They must submit in the future. Successful submission in the future will necessitate the following:
   • a revelation of God's presence with us (verses 13–14a)
   • a realization that God will fight for us (verse 14)
   • worship (verses 14b–15)
   • following God's directions completely, even if it means being thought foolish (Joshua 6:2–5)

Chapter 7 Outline
Christ Appears to Gideon
Judges 6:1–24

After Joshua defeated all of Israel's enemies and established the tribes of Israel in the Promised Land, he died. Instead of appointing another main military leader, God would occasionally raise up men and women who were called judges to lead segments of the Israelites against local enemies. The reason they had to fight these enemies was due to their own disobedience at times. Nevertheless, God was gracious and provided them with the necessary leadership to get them back on track.

The period of the judges is known as one of the lowest times in Israel's history. The last verse of the book of Judges says it all: "In those days Israel had no king. Each man did what he considered to be right" (Judges 21:25). The cycles began with rebellion, which resulted in retribution. Then God would raise up one of the judges to call people back to Him. This resulted in repentance and restoration.

1. Rebellion (verse 1a)
2. Retribution (verses 1b–6a)
3. Repentance (verses 6b–10)
4. Restoration (verses 11–24)

Cowardly Gideon was threshing a small amount of wheat in a wine press, hiding from the enemy, the Midianites, who would come and raid Israel, taking whatever they wanted. Jesus appeared to Gideon, addressing him as a "mighty warrior" (v. 12). He sent Gideon to save Israel, infusing him with courage as he went.

Lessons from This Christophany

- God sees us as we can be, not as we are.
- God is still there when we feel abandoned.
- God delivers us from overwhelming odds (Judges 7).

Chapter 8 Outline
Christ Appears to Manoah's Wife
Judges 13

1. The Rebellion (Judges 13:1a)

2. The Retribution (Judges 13:1b)

3. The Revelation (Judges 13:2–20)
   o Christophany 1—Verses 2–8
   o Christophany 2—Verses 9–20

4. The Realization (Judges 13:21–23)
   o They learned they would have a son by God's miraculous intervention.
   o They learned that his birth was announced by the preincarnate Son of God.

Lessons from This Christophany

What about us today? Should we stand ready to serve God? Most definitely! Of course, we shouldn't expect a visit from an angel with a similar message, because we have Christ in our hearts, and we have His written Word. We have opportunities daily to serve God in many ways. Paul told the Ephesians to "make the most of every opportunity" (Eph. 5:16). How do we stand ready to serve God?

1. We have to be strong spiritually.
2. We have to put God first in our lives.
3. We have to be well equipped.

NOTES

1   W. Howard Doane, *The Silver Spray* (Cincinnati, Ohio: John Church, 1868), number 20.

2   Charles Lee Feinberg, "theophany" in *Holman Bible Dictionary, ed. Trent C. Butler (Nashville: Holman Bible Publishers, 1991), 1338.*

3   Ibid.

4   Merrill C. Tenney, ed., *The Zondervan Pictorial Bible Dictionary* (Grand Rapids: Zondervan Publishing House, 1963), 846.

5   W. E. Vine, *An Expository Dictionary of Biblical Words (New York: Thomas Nelson Publishers, 1984), 57.*

6   Mark Driscoll, *Jesus in the Old Testament* (www.patheos.com/blogs/markdriscoll/so17/03/Jesus-in-the-old-testament-part-4christophanies/).

7   John Walvoord, *Jesus Christ Our Lord* (Chicago: Moody Bible Institute), 54.

8   Horace Bushnell, *Sermons for the New Life, (New York: Charles Scribner, 1858) 22.*

9   James S. Hewitt, ed., *Illustrations Unlimited (Wheaton: Tyndale House Publishers, 1988), 304–305.*

10   John MacArthur, *The MacArthur Study Bible* (Wheaton: Crossway Publishers, 2010), 38–39.

11   Leo Tolstoy, *Three Methods of Reform* (Pamphlets: Translated from the Russian, *1900).*

12   Harold Sherman, *How to Turn Failure into Success (New York: A. Thomas Company, 1916), 138.*

13   Stan Toler and Martha Bolton, *God Has Never Failed Me, But He's Sure Scared Me to Death A Few Times (Tulsa: Honor Books, 1998), 162.*

14   Ewald Plass, *What Luther Says* (St. Louis: *Concordia Publishing House, 1959), 391–404.*

15   Henry F. Henrichs, ed., *Sunshine Magazine* (Litchfield, Illinois: Sunshine Press, January 1984), 16.

16 William R. Nicoll, *Judges: In the Expositor's Bible Commentary* (Grand Rapids: Zondervan, 2004), 243.

17 Merrill C. Tenney, ed., *The Zondervan Pictorial Bible Dictionary* (Grand Rapids: Zondervan Publishing House, 1967) 575.

Printed in the United States
By Bookmasters